Anglican
Young
People's
Dictionary

Anglican Young
People's
Dictionary

June A. English

Illustrations by
Dorothy Thompson Perez

MOREHOUSE PUBLISHING
A Continuum imprint
HARRISBURG • LONDON • NEW YORK

Morehouse Publishing, P.O. Box 1321, Harrisburg, PA 17105
Morehouse Publishing, The Tower Building, 11 York Road,
   London SE1 7NX
Morehouse Publishing is a Continuum imprint.

Page design by Beth Oberholtzer

Library of Congress Cataloging-in-Publication Data
English, June, 1955-
      Anglican young people's dictionary / June English.
        p.   cm.
      ISBN 0-8192-1985-1
      1. Episcopal Church–Dictionaries–Juvenile literature.
2. Anglican Communion–Dictionaries–Juvenile literature.
I. Title.
BX5007.E54 2004
283'.03–dc22
                                                2004001380
Printed in the United States of America
04   05   06   07   08   09   6   5   4   3   2   1

Introduction

This dictionary is like any other dictionary you might find at home or at school—useful for looking up the meanings of words you don't understand. But this dictionary gives you something more than just definitions in alphabetical order. By helping you explore the rich language of our Church, it can help you define what it means to be an Anglican.

Much of the "Anglican language" is hard to understand—after all, we don't use words like "vestry" or "curate" in our everyday conversations with family and friends. Many church words come from the ancient languages of Latin and Greek, which were spoken during early Christian times. Though these words may have fallen out of use in the secular world, they're still part of the world of the Church. Using this dictionary, you'll learn the origins of many of these words, and get a sense of why—and how—we still use them in worship today.

On a deeper level, the words in this dictionary offer a history of the Anglican faith. A remarkable number of words in Anglican terminology trace their origins to the earliest days of the Christian

Church. In these early times the word *Christian* could hardly be spoken without fear and a *martyr* was something Christians could not only embrace as an idea, but see as a real possibility. The words used in the Church today may sometimes seem ancient and difficult, but they take us back to the times when Christ and his apostles walked the earth. They remind us of his message of hope to the world and connect us with his earliest followers.

Though religious words may be difficult to understand at first, they can be the key to a deeper understanding of your faith and the way you practice it. By looking up unfamiliar words, and using them as you talk about and explore your Church, you can widen the boundaries of your faith.

How to Use This Dictionary

The Anglican Young People's Dictionary is arranged alphabetically. Most terms are defined next to the word, although some terms will direct you to another word for a definition. Certain words include diagrams to show visual details pertinent to the term.

Anglican Young
People's
Dictionary

Acolyte

The word *acolyte* comes from a Greek word meaning "one who serves." Acolytes are lay-people, often teenagers, who serve the church by assisting the priest or deacon during services. Acolytes may carry a banner or incense at the beginning of the worship service. They also assist by lighting and putting out candles, and may receive the offering of the congregation after it is collected. Acolytes may also help the priest prepare the altar, or Lord's Table, for communion. Sometimes acolytes assist the priest or deacon by holding the gospel book during the reading of the text. No matter what acolytes do in any particular worship service, they are there to serve and to show the congregation an example of how to serve others well.

Acolyte

Advent

The Christian year begins with the season of Advent, a word that comes from the Latin *adventus,* or "coming." Starting with the Sunday that falls four weeks before Christmas, the Church prepares for the birth of Jesus. This is also a time of preparation for the Second Advent, or Second Coming of Christ.

That makes this season a time of expectation and waiting, but also of repentance and purification. Gospels and other readings focus on the longing for Jesus, the Messiah, to come into the world. Some Episcopal churches follow the ancient custom of using purple vestments and altar hangings during the Advent season. Purple, the medieval sign of royalty, reminds us that Christ will establish the Kingdom of God on earth. Other churches use deep blue, a symbol of Mary, the mother of Jesus.

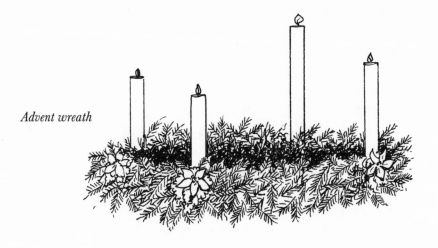

Advent wreath

Advent wreath

The Advent wreath, a circle of evergreens with four candles, is one way to celebrate Advent, both at church and in Christian homes. During the first week of Advent, one candle is lit. During the second week, two candles are lit, and so on until the final week, when all four candles burn brightly. Advent wreaths often have three purple candles and one rose or pink one. The rose candle, lit on the third Sunday of Advent, also known as "Rose" or "Gaudete" Sunday, is a reminder that this is a time of joyful expectation. In the middle of the wreath, many people also include a single white candle as a sign of Christ. This Christ candle is lit on Christmas Eve.

Advent calendar

This is a calendar used to mark the days leading up to Christmas. Commercial Advent calendars usually have twenty-four days—one for each December day before Christmas. Each day is marked by a small flap or door. Each door opens to reveal a picture or message relating to the events of the season. Advent calendars are one good way to remember the significance of the Christmas season.

Alb

The alb is a full-length, loose-fitting garment usually worn by the person celebrating the Mass or Eucharist, as well as by the ministers who are assisting the service. It is most often white or off-white. The alb, whose name comes from a Latin word meaning "white," is often gathered at the waist by a rope or *cincture.*

Alb

All Saints' Day

This feast day, kept in the Anglican Church as well as other churches, celebrates all the Christian saints, both known and unknown. A saint is someone whose life on earth showed the love and compassion of God in a remarkable way. Christians believe that such people continue to be in communion with God after death. On November 1, all the saints are remembered and honored.

All Souls' Day

Since about the fifth century, the Roman Catholic Church has marked the feast of All Souls on November 2 as a day to pray for faithful Christians who have died. Although this feast was discontinued in the Anglican Church with the Protestant Reformation, it was revived in the English 1928 Book of Common Prayer as a way to help Anglicans mourn the deaths of millions of soldiers in World War I. Today the feast is known as the Commemoration of All Faithful Departed.

Altar

The term *altar* comes from words meaning "place of burning." Long ago, altars were used for ritual sacrifice—religious ceremonies in which animals or plants were burned. Today in Anglican churches the altar is the table where we celebrate the Eucharist. Using the word *altar* is a reminder that Jesus' willingness to die was a sacrifice of his life. Since the late 1960s, the altar stands away from the wall as a kind of island. The priest celebrates the Eucharist facing the people.

When it is not being used, the altar is usually covered by a special white linen cloth called an altar

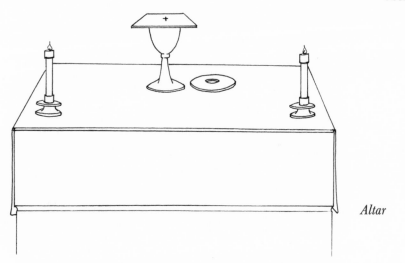

Altar

cloth. During the celebration of the Eucharist, the altar holds the chalice for the wine, the paten for the host, the eucharistic candles, and the altar book, which contains the words spoken by the celebrant during the Eucharist.

Altar Guild

The altar guild is a group of parishioners who prepare the altar for worship. They arrange the items that belong on the altar, including the candles and prayer book as well as preparing bread for the paten and filling the chalice with wine. They make sure that all the altar linens are correctly colored for the season of the church year being observed—purple or blue for Advent, for example, or white for Easter. The altar guild may also take responsibility for church flowers and decorations, particularly for special seasons. Other altar guild duties may include cleaning, sewing, and mending the linens.

Angelus

The Angelus is a prayer that honors the Incarnation, the mystical truth that Jesus, though God, became a human being. It is traditionally recited in the morning, at noon, and in the evening and is often accompanied by the ringing of church bells. The prayer is based on the angel Gabriel's announcement to Mary that she would become the mother of Jesus, son of the Creator. *Angelus* is the Latin word for angel. Some people recite the Angelus as an act of devotion to Mary.

Anglican

An Anglican is a person who is a member of an Anglican church. Anglican churches are members of the Anglican Communion, a worldwide group of churches that are connected through history and belief with the Church of England. Anglicanism is a religion that combines elements of both the Protestant and the Roman Catholic traditions. From the Protestant tradition, Anglicans hold the importance of reading the Bible and forming an individual conscience. From the Roman Catholic tradition, Anglicans maintain the importance of liturgy, tradition, and church organization (or hierarchy). Anglicanism is often thought of as a bridge—or a middle way—between these two traditions.

Anglican Communion

The Anglican Communion, with seventy million members in thirty-eight provinces, is a collection of

Anglican churches around the world. The Anglican Communion headquarters is in London and the spiritual head of the Communion is the Archbishop of Canterbury.

Annunciation

The word *annunciation* comes from the Latin meaning "to announce." It refers to the angel Gabriel's announcement to the Blessed Virgin Mary that she would be the mother of the long-awaited Messiah. With Mary's answer, "Behold the handmaiden of the Lord; be it done unto me according to thy word," Jesus was conceived. Christians commemorate the Annunciation by praying the Magnificat, and celebrating the feast of the Annunciation on March 25.

Anointing

Anointing is the rite of applying holy oil to a person. This act is a sign of God's presence and healing grace. Traditionally, the oils used in anointing come from olives. In the countries of the Mediterranean where Christianity was formed, people depended on oil to prepare food, to give light, and to heal the sick. Today, within the Anglican Church, people are anointed when they are ill; they may also be anointed when they receive the sacraments: baptism, confirmation, and Holy Orders, or ordination. During these ceremonies, the celebrant may anoint people with holy oil known as chrism, a mixture of olive oil and balsam.

Apocrypha

Several ancient holy books are used by the Anglican Church, but are not officially considered part of the Bible. Instead they are known as the Apocrypha, from a Greek word meaning "hidden" or "secret." These books were included in the Septuagint, the Greek translation of the Hebrew Bible used by Jews living outside of Israel during the formative years of Christianity. This Bible was used by early Christians as well.

Because the books are not found in the original Hebrew scriptures, however, Protestant churches during the Reformation of the sixteenth century did not include them in the canon, or official list, of the books of the Bible. They could not be used to determine what Christians should believe, but might offer examples of how to live. Today Anglicans include these writings in a separate section, between the Old and New Testaments, called the Apocrypha. The Apocrypha includes these books: Tobit, Judith, Additions to Esther, Wisdom of Solomon, Sirach or Ecclesiasticus, Baruch, The Letter of Jeremiah, The Prayer of Azariah and the Song of the Three Jews, Susanna, Bel and the Dragon, 1 through 4 Maccabees, Prayer of Manasseh, Psalm 151, and 1 and 2 Esdras.

Apostles

The apostles were the twelve close followers of Jesus. After spending a night in prayer, he personally selected these men, some of whom were fishermen, to carry out his ministry on earth. They accompanied Jesus almost everywhere he traveled.

After Jesus' death and resurrection, the apostles formed the center of the Christian church and, with many other men and women, spread the gospel throughout the Mediterranean world. The word *apostle* comes from a Greek word meaning "messenger." Jesus gave the apostles power to baptize, heal, and forgive sins in his name, and he sent them out to be messengers of his good news.

Some of the apostles had been disciples of John the Baptist and met Jesus at the Jordan River, where John baptized believers. These men were present when Jesus performed his first public miracle at the wedding feast at Cana.

Apostles' Creed

The Apostles' Creed is a summary of the beliefs of the Christian religion. For many years, people believed that it had been written by the apostles soon after they received the Holy Spirit at Pentecost. Now scholars believe that it was probably written around the fourth century. The word *creed* comes from the first word of the statement in Latin, *credo,* which means "I believe." Anglicans recite the creed (either the Apostles' or the Nicene) at every Eucharist.

Apostolic Succession

In the earliest days of the Church, the apostles chose people to help spread the gospel and care for the Church. Through the laying on of hands, the apostles made certain Christians bishops. In turn, the first bishops laid hands on the next generation of bishops, and so on through the centuries, creating an unbroken line of apostolic succession. Today, Anglican bishops can trace their roots back to second-century bishops who were probably successors of the original apostles. Men and women who become bishops in the Anglican Church today receive the laying on of hands from other bishops.

Archbishop

In the Anglican Communion, an archbishop is a bishop whose responsibilities go beyond the geographic boundaries of one diocese. There are two archbishops in England, the Archbishop of Canterbury and the Archbishop of York. In the Episcopal Church in the United States, however, there are no archbishops. Instead, the chief bishop is known as the Presiding Bishop. The Presiding Bishop does not have the duties of a regular bishop, but assumes, instead, the role of an administrator within the church. In the Anglican Church of Canada, the Primate, or head of the church, is an archbishop. There are also four other archbishops who are the leaders of each of the four Canadian church provinces, or large areas of the country.

Archbishop of Canterbury

The Archbishop of Canterbury is head of the Church of England. Traditionally, the Archbishop of Canterbury is also considered the spiritual leader of the entire body of churches within the Anglican Communion. In the year 579, St. Augustine became the first Archbishop of Canterbury.

Archdeacon (look under **Deacon**)

Articles of Religion

The Thirty-nine Articles are brief statements that summarize the beliefs and practices of the Anglican Church in the sixteenth century. Formed during the Reformation in England, the Articles are included in the Book of Common Prayer.

Ash Wednesday

Marking the beginning of Lent, Ash Wednesday is the fortieth weekday before Easter. This day begins a period of fasting and prayer in preparation for Easter. In some churches ashes from burnt palms (from the previous year's Palm Sunday celebration) are traced on the foreheads of Christians. This ancient ritual of penitence has its roots in the Hebrew Bible, where wearing sackcloth and ashes were signs of repentance. Today, however, the imposition of ashes is often omitted, though the Church still calls its members to use the weeks of Lent to purify their spirits and deepen their relationship with God.

Baptism

Baptism is the sacrament of Christian identity, making recipients full members of the Church. In the early Church, people were usually baptized as adults after a long period of preparation. Today, Anglicans are usually baptized as infants, with the parents and godparents speaking on behalf of the

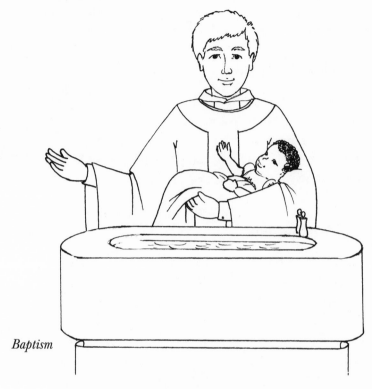

Baptism

child, vowing to share their Christian faith by word and example. The priest or deacon sprinkles water on the child's head and anoints the child's forehead with holy oil.

Spiritually, baptism is the transition from the death of sin to a new life in Christ. Before the birth of Christ, Jews practiced immersion (dunking) in water as a ritual of purification, or spiritual cleansing. The word *baptism* comes from a Greek word meaning "to dip." Jesus himself consented to be baptized by his cousin John in the river Jordan. On this day, John the Baptist, marking a change in what baptism would come to mean, tells the crowd: *I indeed have baptized you with water; but He [Christ] shall baptize you with the Holy Spirit.*

Bible

The Holy Bible is a collection of sixty-six books that contain the Scriptures, or holy writings, of the Jewish and the Christian religions. Anglicans believe that the holy Scriptures contain "all things necessary to salvation." The Bible is separated into two testaments, or covenants, that teach us about God's relationship with people. The Old Testament contains the Hebrew Scriptures, written before the birth of Christ, which tell of the relationship between God and the Jews through histories, law, and prophetic writings. The New Testament contains scriptures written after the life of Christ, describing his ministry and the beginnings of his Church. (Judaism, in general, does not recognize the New Testament as being part of the true Bible.)

Both Jews and Christians believe that the Bible is inspired by God, though persons of different faiths interpret the Bible in different ways. Scholars continue to work with ancient Scripture sources to help us come to a better, fuller understanding of the Bible.

Bishop

The word *bishop* comes from a Greek word for "overseer" or "supervisor." In the Anglican Church, the bishop is the chief priest and pastor of the diocese and symbolically unites the church community with the original apostles. In the early United States,

Bishop

in fact, Episcopal bishops took on the role of missionaries just as the apostles did. They journeyed to the western frontier to establish churches where none existed.

Today the bishop heads the diocese, though many bishops see their role as pastoring church members rather than governing them. Bishops counsel those wishing to become priests or deacons, and also ordain new priests and deacons. They preside at confirmations and they also may baptize and celebrate the Eucharist. Bishops are obliged to visit all the parishes in their diocese regularly.

The authority of the church rests with the bishop. However, bishops do not hold a position of rulership in the church. In the United States, for example, they help determine—and carry out—the rules set by the General Convention, which meets every three years. In Canada, they are members of the General Synod, which also meets every three years. They help guide the church in carrying out the decisions of the synod, which is made up of both lay and ordained people.

The *mitre* (a liturgical headdress) and the *crozier* (a staff resembling a shepherd's crook) are symbols of the bishop's authority and role as principal shepherd-pastor.

Book of Common Prayer

The Book of Common Prayer is the prayer book of the Anglican Church. The first edition was composed in 1549 by Archbishop Thomas Cranmer, who gathered into one book all the worship services of the medieval church. Remarkably for the time, the Book of Common Prayer was written in English, the language of the people, rather than in Latin, which only a few wealthy and educated people could understand. From this point on, clergy and laypeople would use their own language for prayer and worship.

This book provides a basis for worship for all Anglican congregations throughout the world, though there are some variations between prayer books in the various countries of the Anglican Communion. In Canada, for example, there are two worship books in use. One, last revised in 1962, is called the Book of Common Prayer. There is also a Book of Alternative Services, completed in 1985. Both books contain rites for baptism, Eucharist, marriage, burial, and ordination services, as well as the Psalms. All prayer books are revised periodically; in the United States, the most recent revision was adopted in 1979.

The first Anglican-American prayer book was authorized just after the Revolutionary War in 1789. Like the Canadian version, the American Book of Common Prayer contains texts for all the principal church services, as well as the Psalms.

Candlemas

The Feast of the Presentation of Christ in the Temple, also known as Candlemas, is celebrated by the Church on February 2. The feast commemorates Mary and Joseph bringing the infant Christ into the temple for the first time. As reported in the Gospel of Luke, the infant Jesus was recognized as the Messiah by a prophetess, Anna, and a holy man,

Simeon. On Candlemas Day, we bless candles to commemorate Simeon's prayer, in which he calls Jesus "a Light to enlighten the nations." This traditional blessing of the candles during this feast became popular during the eleventh century.

Candles

Many different types of candles are used in church services, including altar candles, which are lit during the celebration of the Eucharist. Some churches also use votive candles that often serve as symbols of a personal request. (The word *votive* comes from the Latin word for promise.) During Advent, the candles of the Advent wreath are used to mark the time leading up to Christmas.

The most important Church candle is the Paschal, or Easter, candle. Tall and white, this candle is often decorated with a cross and the letters alpha and omega, the beginning and ending letters of the Greek alphabet. Representing the light of the risen Christ, this candle is lit from a new fire at the beginning of the Easter vigil and provides light during the entire Easter season. It may also be lit during the celebration of baptism, or during a burial service.

Canon Law

Canon is simply the Latin word for "rule." Canon law is a set of rules that govern the Anglican Church. Each national church within the Anglican Communion has its own set of canon laws. Each diocese has its own canon laws as well, although these laws cannot conflict with the canon law of the national church. In the United States and Canada, canon law may be modified every three years at the nationwide meetings (General Convention in the United States and General Synod in Canada).

Canon of Ministers

This is an Anglican, usually a member of the clergy, who holds a position at a cathedral church, such as "canon for religious formation." There are also canons who are not part of the cathedral's paid staff but hold the honorary title for their contribution to the life of a diocese.

Canticle

Canticle comes from the Latin word for "song." It is a prayer from the Bible that is often chanted or sung. Anglicans pray two canticles every day in the Daily Office: the Canticle of Mary, or the *Magnificat,* in the evening, and the Canticle of Zechariah, or *Benedictus,* in the morning.

Cassock

This ankle-length robe fastened at the neck is the standard vestment of priests and deacons. It is also worn by lay ministers. The cassock was originally used as street dress in ancient Rome. The traditional color of cassock is black, but in hotter, tropical climates, white is often used. Bishops wear purple cassocks.

Cathedral

A cathedral is the main or principal church of a diocese. Many important services, such as the ordination of priests and deacons, take place in a diocesan cathedral. It typically holds the *cathedra,* a special chair for the bishop. Often, a cathedral is a large and elaborate building, but it doesn't have to be; sometimes it is simply the parish church of the bishop.

Catechism

Catechisms are books or pamphlets of instructions, in question-and-answer format, for those preparing for the rite of confirmation. The word *catechism* comes from a Greek word meaning "to teach by word of mouth."

The catechism included in the Book of Common Prayer contains a brief summary of the beliefs of Anglicans. In the United States, the catechism is officially called "An Outline of the Faith." From time to time, these catechisms may be revised.

Catholic

Catholic literally means "universal" or "occurring everywhere," and it refers to the faith that all Christians share in common. The term *catholic* is often used to mean Roman Catholic, but it is an equally correct term for Anglicans and several other Christian denominations, which accept both Christian tradition and Holy Scripture as their foundation. In the Nicene and Apostles' Creeds, the word *catholic* is used to define the Universal Church.

Celebrant

The celebrant is the leader of a worship service. The person who leads the Eucharist is a priest or a bishop; the Daily Office may be led by a member of the clergy or a layperson.

Centrum (look under Church Plan)

Chalice

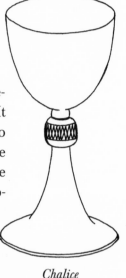

The chalice is the cup that holds the wine conse- crated during the celebration of the Eucharist. It represents the cup that Jesus blessed and gave to his disciples during the Last Supper. The chalice is traditionally silver or gold, but may also be made of ceramic, pewter, glass, or another appro- priate material.

At the Eucharist, the person who offers the chalice containing the consecrated wine to worshipers is called the chalice bearer.

Chalice

Chancel

In traditionally designed churches, the chancel is the area around the altar. The chancel often includes a space for the church choir. In many churches, there are three steps leading from the main part of the church to the chancel.

Chapel

The word *chapel* has two meanings. It may refer to a part of a building, such as a school or hospital, which is used for religious purposes; or, it may refer to a section of a larger church that has its own altar and is used for services or prayer. Frequently, these "side chapels" are dedicated to a saint. If they are dedicated to the Blessed Virgin Mary, they are often called a "Lady Chapel." Small churches in rural areas are sometimes referred to as chapels.

Chicago-Lambeth Quadrilateral

In 1886, the General Convention of the Episcopal Church met in Chicago and wrote down the four points that form the foundation of the Christian faith. In 1888 the bishops of the Anglican Communion met in Lambeth, England, and adopted a slightly revised version of the four points. They are:

1. The Scriptures of the Bible contain "all things necessary to salvation."

2. The Apostles' Creed and the Nicene Creed are "the sufficient statement of the Christian faith."

3. The two sacraments ordained by Christ are baptism and the Eucharist.

4. The "historic episcopate" traces the authority of the bishops back to the apostles.

The Chicago-Lambeth Quadrilateral has been the foundation for discussions about unity among the many branches of the Christian faith.

Christian Symbols

During the two thousand years of the Christian era, many symbols have evolved to illustrate Christian

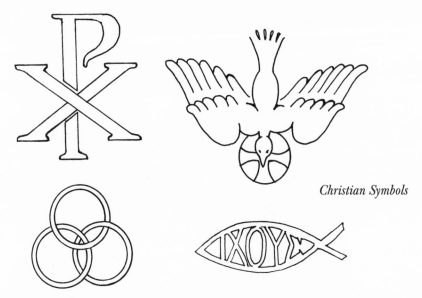

Christian Symbols

beliefs and ideas. These images are often used on church buildings and decorations, as well as on vestments. The cross itself is the primary symbol of Christianity; its design varies from culture to culture.

Many other Christian symbols are based on Latin or Greek letters. The first two letters of the word Christ in Greek are often used in Christian art; we refer to this symbol as the Chi Rho. Another letter-based symbol is INRI. These letters were part of the initials of a sign Pontius Pilate wrote out and put on the cross where Jesus was crucified. The sign read: *Jesus of Nazareth, King of the Jews.*

The fish symbol for Christ and Christians is also taken from initials—in this case the Greek words for Jesus Christ, Son of God, Savior. These letters, ΙΧΟΥΣ, spell the Greek word for fish. Another Christian symbol uses the Greek letters alpha and omega, the first and last letters of the Greek alphabet. We use this symbol because the writer of the

Book of Revelation refers to Christ as the Alpha and the Omega, the beginning and the end.

Christmas

Also known as the Feast of the Incarnation or the Feast of the Nativity, Christmas is the celebration of the birth of Christ, the Messiah and Savior promised by God to his people. The traditions and celebrations on and around this feast day vary throughout Christian denominations and cultures.

Christmas was first observed on December 25 around the year 336. This day was likely chosen because it fell on the pagan feast of the sun. Christmas Day is the beginning, not the end, of the Christmas season. It marks the first of the twelve days of Christmas, culminating on January 5, the eve of the Feast of the Epiphany, which celebrates the visit of the Magi and the epiphany, or "showing" of Christ to the non-Jewish world.

The exact timing of Jesus' birth is not known, although the announcement of that birth is described eloquently in the gospel of Luke, repeating the words of rejoicing angels to shepherds (Luke 2:10–11 KJV):

> Fear not: for behold, I bring you good tidings of great joy which shall be to all people. For unto you is born this day in the city of David a Savior, which is Christ the Lord.

Church Calendar

The church year is divided into six seasons: Advent, Christmas, the period following the Epiphany, Lent,

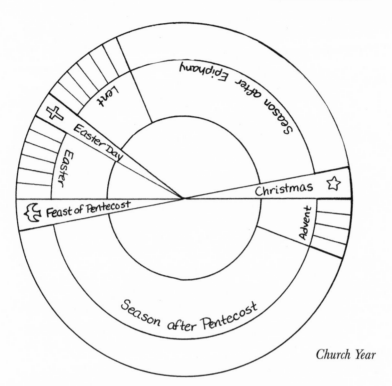

Church Year

Easter, and the period after Pentecost, often called "Ordinary Time." The two major Christian feasts of Easter and Christmas roughly divide the year.

Advent, the period of preparation leading up to Christmas, begins four Sundays before December 25. The Christmas season lasts for twelve days, from December 25 to January 5 or to the Epiphany, which is celebrated on January 6th. The season following the Epiphany continues to Ash Wednesday, the beginning of Lent. Lent lasts for forty weekdays and six Sundays. The date of Easter changes from year to year: It's celebrated on the first Sunday on or after the first full moon of spring, which officially begins March 21. The season of Pentecost begins fifty days after Easter and continues until Advent.

The Scripture passages read on Sundays through-out the church year take Anglicans through the life and ministry of Jesus. Other special days remind Christians of the lives of saints, such as Peter and Paul, or fundamental beliefs of the Christian faith, such as the Holy Trinity.

Church Plan

Traditional church buildings are divided into two spaces: a nave, where the congregation sits, and a choir, where the clergy, choir, and servers sit. The altar is located in the choir. In more modern churches, the nave and the choir are combined in a single space called the centrum. This single-room approach helps to unify the people and the clergy.

Churches often have a separate space with its own altar known as a chapel.

Ciborium

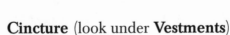

The ciborium is a lidded container used to hold the unconsecrated wafers as they are brought to the altar at the Offertory. Following the conse-cration of the wafers, they are held in the cibo-rium as they are distributed to the people during communion.

Ciborium

Cincture (look under Vestments)

Collects

Collects are short, simple prayers, usually just one sentence long, that contain three parts: an invocation of God's name; a petition, or request, to God; and the praise of God. Prayers called collects were used in the early Christian churches. These *collected* prayers were said over the gathered assembly before they set out to the site where the Eucharist would be held. A famous collect is one written by Thomas Cranmer in the original Book of Common Prayer:

> Almighty and everlasting God, which hateth nothing which thou hast made, and dost forgive the sins of all them that be penitent, create and make in us new and contrite hearts, that we worthily lamenting our sins and acknowledging our wretchedness, may obtain of thee, the God of all, mercy, perfect remission and forgiveness, through Jesus Christ.

This collect—in more modern wording—is still used by the Anglican Church today.

Colors (Liturgical)

The colors of church decorations, vestments, and altar linens change according to the seasons of the church year. Violet, or sometimes blue, is used for Advent and Lent—times of expectation and purification. During the Christmas season and on the feast of the Epiphany, the church color changes to white, symbolizing renewal and joy. Beginning on the third Sunday of Epiphany, the church color becomes green, as it does during the season of Pentecost. White is used again during the season of Easter, another feast of new life, as well as for weddings and funerals and some saints' feast days.

Martyrs are commemorated with red, a symbol of the shedding of blood. Red is also used for Holy

Week and the feast of Pentecost, when the color symbolizes the flames of the Holy Spirit.

Though these color guides apply generally, some communities make exceptions. The Episcopal Church in the U.S.A. requires no particular system of color. Instead, churches rely on tradition and personal choice. For instance, some parishes use red on Good Friday while others use black to signify profound loss and sorrow.

Communicant

A communicant in the Anglican Church is someone who has received communion (Holy Eucharist) at least three times within the past year and who has been "faithful in working, praying, and giving" for the benefit of the Church and the Kingdom of God. Parishes and missions often keep lists of their members and communicants. Members of the vestry, as well as others who hold offices in the church, are required to be communicants.

Communion (look under Eucharist)

Confirmation

Confirmation is a sacramental rite that is linked to baptism. In confirmation, a person confirms the early vows made on his or her behalf by parents and godparents. The rite is usually administered to young people around the age of twelve, although the recent trend is toward confirming young people in their mid-to-late teens.

Confirmation also commemorates the gift of the Holy Spirit promised by Jesus to his disciples after his resurrection and received by them on Pentecost. This gift of the Spirit, passed on to other disciples through the laying on of hands, echoes through the history of Christianity. Today's bishops pray that the Holy Spirit be strengthened in the persons being confirmed, helping them to live out the faith of the apostles.

Consecration

Consecration is the act of making something sacred, or holy. During the celebration of the Eucharist, the bread and wine are consecrated, becoming the body and blood of Jesus. Christ himself first performed this act of consecration during his last supper with the apostles. During this meal, Jesus asked those gathered to continue this consecration and feast in memory of him.

Consecration also refers to the act of elevating priests to the office of bishop. The term can also be used for a church building, which a priest or bishop may consecrate when it is first built.

Creed

A creed is a statement of belief. In the Anglican Church, the Apostles' Creed and the Nicene Creed contain the Church's most important beliefs. The word comes the statement in Latin, *credo,* or "I believe." See separate entries for Apostles' Creed and Nicene Creed.

Crosses

Cross

The cross is the most recognizable symbol of Christianity. Its simple form represents the cross used by the Romans to execute Jesus Christ. In a more complex way, the horizontal pole of the cross represents the humanity of Jesus; the vertical pole signifies his divinity. Most importantly, the cross symbolizes Jesus' sacrifice for humanity, and the redemption of humankind through his death and resurrection.

Earlier Christian churches were often built in the form of a cross and many cathedrals maintain that form. Modern churches usually have a large cross behind the altar and crosses are frequently carried in church processions. This powerful sign is used in religious art, in the liturgy, on church decorations and vestments, and in physical annointings and blessings.

Many different forms of the Christian cross have evolved over the years. Some represent particular aspects of Christian history and some reflect different cultures.

Curate

This word comes from the Latin word meaning "to care." A curate is an assistant priest who helps the senior priest care for the needs of the people of a parish. Usually, a curate is a recent seminary graduate who gains additional training and experience by assisting a more experienced priest.

Daily Office

The daily offices are prayer services used in worship each day. These combinations of prayers contain collects, scripture readings, prayers, psalms, canticles, the creed, confession, and petition. They can be prayed in church, led by a priest, deacon, or layperson, or prayed at home by individuals or families. The Daily Office is included in the Books of Common Prayer and Alternative Services. There are daily offices for morning, noon, evening, and "compline," the last prayer hour of the day. These are based on the practice of monks and nuns praying together at various times throughout the day and night.

Dalmatic (look under Vestments)

Deacon

Deacons are men and women ordained within the Anglican Communion of Churches to serve the congregation. Deacons become familiar with the needs of the people of the parish, then communicate those needs to the bishop and the wider Church. During the Eucharist, deacons perform a variety of tasks, such as reading the gospel, preparing the altar, offering the prayers of the people, and dismissing the congregation.

The appointment of deacons is specifically referred to in the Acts of the Apostles (6:1–7). When

Deacon wearing a Dalmatic

it became clear that the church community needed more assistance than the apostles themselves could provide, seven deacons were chosen to help tend to the needs of the poor.

Deacons wear special vestments including an identifying stole over the left shoulder and a knee-length tunic called a dalmatic.

Those who are preparing for the priesthood are first ordained as transitional deacons and spend about a year in that role, working in parishes, before becoming priests.

An archdeacon is a priest or deacon who serves as a special assistant to the bishop.

Diocese

Diocese is the name given by the Church to a particular geographic area. It is the main unit of organization and administration in the Anglican Church—the word comes to us from the Greek word meaning "to administer," or "to keep house." Each diocese consists of a number of parishes and is overseen by a bishop and a diocesan council, a group of lay and clerical members.

Easter

The celebration of Easter, commemorating Christ's resurrection from the dead, is the oldest and most important celebration in the Christian Church. It begins with the Great Vigil of Easter, the time from dusk on Holy Saturday to sunrise on Easter morning, a tradition that has been practiced since the fourth century. The Vigil starts with the lighting of the Easter fire, from which the new Easter candle is lit, and ends with the celebration of the Eucharist and the baptism of new Christians.

The exact date upon which Easter is celebrated changes from year to year, but always falls between March 22 and April 25.

Ecumenism

Ecumenism is a movement established to bring Christian churches together. This specifically means finding beliefs that the churches agree on and using that common ground to establish closer, more meaningful relationships. See also Lutheran-Episcopal Concordat. See also World Council of Churches.

Epiphany

The Epiphany is the celebration of the visit of the wise men, or magi, to the child Jesus. The word *epiphany* comes from a Greek word meaning "appearance" or "manifestation": it marks the moment when Christ was revealed not just to his own Jewish community but to the world beyond. Epiphany is celebrated on January 6, the day that marks the end of the Christmas season.

Episcopal

The Episcopal Church is officially known as the Episcopal Church in the United States of America.

The word *Episcopal* comes from the Latin word meaning "bishop," signifying that the Church's authority derives from bishops, successors of the apostles. The beginnings of the Episcopal Church in America go back to the settlement in Jamestown, Virginia in 1607. A member of the Anglican Communion, the Episcopal Church has 2.3 million members in more than one hundred dioceses and nearly 7,500 parishes. Members of the church are known as Episcopalians.

Eucharist

The word Eucharist comes from the Greek word meaning "thanksgiving." It is a worship service based upon Jesus' Passover supper with the apostles before his trial and execution. At this traditional Jewish feast Christ consecrated bread and wine and asked the apostles to repeat these acts "in memory of me." The Eucharist has been celebrated in Christian churches for two thousand years.

The Eucharist is also called Holy Communion, Mass, and the Lord's Supper. It is divided into two main parts: the Liturgy of the Word, during which portions of the Bible are read and a sermon is preached; and the Liturgy of the Eucharist, during which the bread and wine are consecrated and shared.

Feast Days

Feast days are days of celebration within the church. Officially, they include all Sundays and saints' days. The major feast days, however, are Easter, Pentecost,

Christmas, Epiphany, and All Saints' Day. On these days, special prayers and vestment colors are sometimes used for worship services. In many parishes, special traditions are associated with feast days.

General Convention

The General Convention is a national assembly of the Episcopal Church that meets every three years to set policies and determine budgets for the Church in the United States. The Convention consists of two houses: the House of Bishops, which includes all bishops, including those who are retired; and the House of Deputies, made up of four clergy and four laypeople from each diocese. Together, the houses consider questions ranging from revisions to the Prayer Book to matters of theology and ethics.

As in the United States Congress, all actions must be passed by both Houses.

Other national churches of the Anglican Communion call their meetings by different names. In the Anglican Church of Canada, for instance, the General Synod meets every three years to discuss church policies. The General Synod, like the General Convention, sets policies, determines priorities, and approves budgets. Bishops, clergy, and laypeople from all dioceses meet together to discuss and vote on the issues.

Good Friday

The passion and death of Jesus Christ are remembered in solemn reverence on Good Friday. This is the only day of the church year when the Eucharist is not celebrated. Instead the altar and church are stripped bare and the crosses and any pictures or statues may be removed or covered with cloths. Special devotions are practiced, such as the Stations of the Cross, and the passion narrative from the Gospel of John (the story of Jesus' suffering and death) is read.

Gospel

The word *gospel* comes from the Greek word meaning "good news." The gospels are the stories of Jesus' life and teachings as recorded in the New Testament of the Bible. There are four separate gospels: Matthew, Mark, Luke, and John. Mark's gospel is the most basic of the gospels and many scholars think it was written first. Many of the stories and parables appear in more than one gospel, though some episodes occur only once. The first three gospels (Matthew, Mark, and Luke) have similar content and are known as the Synoptic, or similar, Gospels. *Synoptic* comes from Greek words meaning "seeing with one eye."

During the Eucharist service, the gospel is read by a deacon or priest.

Gradual

The gradual is the Bible text read during the Eucharist, between the reading of the Epistle and the gospel. Its name, Latin for "step," comes from the fact that the choir used to sing this text from the altar steps.

Holy Week

In preparation for the feast of Easter, Holy Week recalls the events leading up to Christ's crucifixion and resurrection. It is the most important week in the Christian year.

Holy Week begins with Palm Sunday, which commemorates Jesus' public entrance into Jerusalem. Maundy Thursday marks Jesus' last Passover supper with the apostles, along with his betrayal into the hands of his enemies. On the following day, Good Friday, Christians remember Jesus' suffering and execution on the cross. On Holy Saturday at dusk, the waiting period known as the Easter Vigil begins. Dawn on Sunday brings the celebration of Christ's return to life and the joy of the resurrection, which we recall on Easter.

Host

The host is the consecrated bread of Holy Communion. In most Anglican churches, the priest consecrates a small, thin wafer, although some churches use baked bread. The word *host* comes from the Latin word for "sacrifice."

Hymns

Hymns are songs to God—sacred or spiritual poems set to music. Parishioners sing hymns during worship services and other occasions. Biblical passages—including psalms—are also sometimes set to music, but these are not always considered hymns.

Diverse people have composed hymns through the centuries. Some hymns, such as "O Gladsome Light" and "Hymn to the Holy Trinity," have survived from the earliest days of the Church. One of the most famous Christian hymns, "Amazing Grace," was written by John Newton, a slave ship master who later became an Anglican priest. It is thought that the melody for this hymn came from the chants sung by the slaves as they rowed in captivity across the ocean.

Incarnation (look under Christmas)

Incense

Some Anglican churches use incense in their worship services. Incense is made from scented gums of trees or plants. During church services and processions, these are burned together with charcoal in a thurible, a container with holes that can be swung back and forth. As the incense and charcoal burn together, the scented smoke moves through the air, symbolizing the prayers of the people rising up to God.

The use of incense in worship dates back to Old Testament days. Eastern Christian churches first used it in the fourth century during the rule of Constantine.

Intercessions

Also known as Prayers of the People, these are prayers for the needs of the community and the world. They are offered during Morning and Evening

Prayer and at the Eucharist, immediately after the recitation of the creed. This is one of the oldest forms of prayer used in the Christian church. It provides an opportunity for people to petition God through prayer during the church service.

Intinction

This term describes one way of receiving the Eucharist—by dipping the communion wafer into the consecrated wine.

Invitatory

As the name suggests, this is a psalm or other song that invites the worshiper into a service. In the Anglican Daily Office, each Morning Prayer service begins with an invitatory.

Kyrie

Kyrie eleison are the Greek words for "Lord, have mercy." This prayer is often recited in the original Greek, but even when it is prayed in English it is referred to by its Greek name. It is recited just after the opening prayers of the Eucharist service.

Laity

Laity comes from the Greek word *laios,* which means "the people." The laity are church members who are not ordained. In their ministry, or call to service, however, they have much in common with the clergy. Laypersons, too, are called to represent Christ—not only in the Church, but in the world where they work and live.

Lambeth Conference

Every ten years, the bishops of the Anglican Communion meet in Canterbury, England, to discuss issues that affect the Church and the world. Discussion topics range from policies of the Church to questions of war, peace, and politics that affect the wider world. The conference is named after the Archbishop of Canterbury's official residence in London, Lambeth Palace. The first meeting took place there in 1867 as a result of a request from the Anglican Church in Canada.

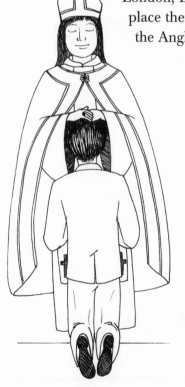

Laying on of Hands

In the gospels, Jesus often touches those he heals, lifting up a woman to straighten her spine, and touching the eyes of a blind man to restore his vision. As his apostles began their ministry in his name, they continued to lay hands on those who were sick, or seeking forgiveness for sin, as part of Christian healing. Today, the laying on of hands is used in the church as a spiritual—and sometimes physical—healing practice. Priests lay on hands during baptism, reconciliation, and anointing of the sick; bishops do so when they administer confirmation and Holy Orders.

Laying on of hands

Lay Eucharistic Minister (look under Lay Minister)

Lay Minister

A lay minister is not ordained, but nevertheless works closely with the Church and its programs. Lay ministers may be paid staff members or may work as volunteers. They must receive specific permission (license) to perform their ministries from the local bishop.

Lay eucharistic ministers are persons who are licensed to distribute bread and wine to the people during Holy Communion. These ministers also deliver communion, previously consecrated by a priest during the Eucharist, to people confined to their homes, or to those who live in nursing homes and hospitals, connecting them to the congregation.

A lay reader is a person who is licensed to conduct services that do not involve consecrating the Eucharist, bestowing a blessing, or absolving sin. For example, a lay reader may lead the Daily Office. Other lay ministries include those of lay preachers, pastoral leaders, and Christian educators.

Lectionary

The lectionary is a book that lists all the Bible passages used during worship services throughout the church year. In the United States, most Anglicans use the lectionaries in the Book of Common Prayer, while in other countries, including Canada, they use the Revised Common Lectionary (R.C.L.). The R.C.L. is also followed by other Christian denominations, such as the Methodists and the Lutherans.

The lectionary includes readings for Sunday services, as well as for other special days such as Christmas, Ash Wednesday, and Epiphany.

For Anglicans, there is a separate lectionary that contains the Bible readings used in the Daily Office. This lectionary, also found in the American and Canadian Books of Common Prayer, as well as the Book of Alternative Services, is arranged in two-year cycles, Year 1 and Year 2.

Lector

A lector, usually a layperson, reads the lessons before the reading of the gospel. A lector may be appointed to serve for a specific reading or the church may have a group of lectors who take turns reading the Bible at worship services. Lectors may also lead the Prayers of the People.

Lent

Lent is the Church season following Ash Wednesday and leading up to Holy Week and Easter. It is a season of self-examination and repentance when Christians reflect on their lives and try to deepen their relationships with God. Some people make physical sacrifices such as giving up a favorite activity or food, while others concentrate on prayer or good works. The season also recalls the time of Christ's fasting in the wilderness, when he separated himself from the world to be closer to his Father.

Because Sundays are considered feast days in the Church, traditional fasting and other Lenten disciplines aren't practiced on these days during Lent.

Lesser Feasts and Fasts

Throughout the Church year, we remember the people and events that make up our heritage as Christians. Major feast days recall events in the time of Christ, such as Christmas, Easter, and Epiphany. Lesser Feasts and Fasts are days that commemorate saints who lived after Jesus, people who provided examples of how to live a Christian life. Some of the lesser feasts and fasts days honor St. Patrick (March 17), St. Benedict (July 11), St. Margaret of Scotland (November 16), and St. Nicholas (December 6). The names of these saints, one for each day of the year, are listed in the Proper for the Lesser Feasts and Fasts, which also contains scripture readings and biographies.

Lessons

The lessons are selections from the Bible that are read during worship services. These are used during the Eucharist and the Daily Office. Each service contains an Old Testament reading, a psalm, a New Testament reading, and a gospel reading.

The lessons begin with the Church year on the first Sunday of Advent. The readings are arranged in three-year cycles, called Year A, Year B, and Year C. There are four readings for each Sunday and feast day: one from the Psalms, one from the Old Testament, one from an Epistle or Letter, and one from the Gospel. During the season of Easter, the Old Testament reading is replaced with a second reading from the Acts of the Apostles. Year A's gospel readings are drawn mainly from Matthew, Year B's from Mark, and Year C's from Luke.

Liturgy

Liturgy, which comes from a Greek term meaning "the work of the people," refers to the public worship of God. Examples of liturgies are the Eucharist and the Daily Office.

Liturgy of the Table

The Liturgy of the Table is the second part of the Eucharist service, in which the people meet Christ through the consecrated bread and wine of Holy Communion. This part of the service extends from the Offertory to the dismissal, or the end of the service. During the Liturgy of the Table, the priest consecrates the bread and wine and distributes them during Holy Communion.

Liturgy of the Word

The first part of the Eucharist service is called the Liturgy of the Word; it focuses on listening to the Word of God through the Scriptures. This part of the liturgy includes readings from the Old and New Testaments, the Psalms, and the Gospel, followed by a sermon often connected to the message of the readings. The Liturgy of the Word usually includes the recitation of the creed, as well as the intercessions, or prayers of the people.

Lord's Prayer

This is the prayer that Jesus taught the apostles. It has been used in Christian worship since the fourth

century. Today we recite it as we prepare for communion during the Eucharist service. The Lord's
Prayer is included in the Book of Common Prayer
in two versions. Here is the traditional version:

Our Father, who art in heaven,
   hallowed be thy Name,
   thy kingdom come,
   thy will be done,
      on earth as it is in heaven.
Give us this day our daily bread.
And forgive us our trespasses,
   as we forgive those
      who trespass against us.
And lead us not into temptation,
   but deliver us from evil.
For thine is the kingdom,
   and the power, and the glory,
   for ever and ever. Amen.

Lord's Supper (look under **Eucharist** or **Mass**)

Lutheran-Episcopal Concordat

In 2000, the Evangelical Lutheran Church in America and the Episcopal Church in the U.S.A. signed
an agreement or concordat allowing the churches to
share in one another's ministry and sacraments. This
means that while each Church will retain its own
identity and customs, clergy from one Church can
preside at the liturgy of the other, and Episcopalians
and Lutherans may receive communion in one
another's churches. This concordat was reached after
years of study and prayer, during which those

involved examined the beliefs, liturgies, and other practices of each Church. The concordat is an important step toward Christian unity. Similar agreements have been reached between other Anglican and Lutheran national churches. In Canada, for example, the Evangelical Lutheran Church in Canada and the Anglican Church of Canada entered into full communion with one another in 2001, when they signed the Waterloo Declaration. Both churches voted to do this at national meetings held at the same time in the city of Waterloo. This agreement allows the two churches to work more closely together. For example, Anglican and Lutheran clergy may now serve in each other's parishes.

Magnificat

The Magnificat is also known as the Song of Mary. It is one of two canticles (or prayer-songs) used during evening prayer. The Magnificat is based on Mary's words to Elizabeth when she reveals she has conceived the child of God. The passage is recorded in the Gospel of Luke:

> My soul proclaims the greatness of the Lord,
> my spirit rejoices in God my Savior;
>> for he has looked with favor on his lowly servant.
> From this day all generations will call me blessed:
>> the Almighty has done great things for me,
>> and holy is his Name.
> He has mercy on those who fear him
>> in every generation.
> He has shown the strength of his arm,
>> he has scattered the proud in their conceit.

He has cast down the mighty from their thrones,
   and has lifted up the lowly.
He has filled the hungry with good things,
   and the rich he has sent away empty.
He has come to the help of his servant Israel,
   for he has remembered his promise of mercy,
The promise he made to our fathers,
   to Abraham and his children for ever.

The word *magnificat* comes from the Latin word for magnify, which means "to glorify or to praise." The naming of the prayer comes from the words that begin the traditional version: "My soul doth magnify the Lord."

Mass

Mass is the traditional word for the celebration of the Eucharist. The word comes from the Latin phrase formerly used to dismiss worshipers at the end of the service: *Ite, missa est* (Go, it is finished). Masses may be designated *low* or *high* depending on the number of clergy participating and how complex the liturgy is.

Matins

This word comes from the French word for "morning"; in medieval monasteries, matin was used to denote the first prayers of the day. Today the divine office of morning prayer is still sometimes called matins.

Matrimony

Holy Matrimony is one of the sacramental rites of Anglicans. Through Holy Matrimony, the joined couple asks for God's assistance, the blessing of the Church, and the support of the community, as they begin their lives together.

Maundy Thursday

Maundy Thursday is the Thursday of Holy Week, the day we remember Jesus' last supper with his apostles. The word *Maundy* comes from the Latin word for "commandment." On this day, Jesus gave two commandments to his apostles: to love one another (John 13:34) and to celebrate the Eucharist in his memory (Luke 22:19). In Anglican churches, the day is often marked with a special Eucharist service, including foot washing—a re-enactment of Christ's washing of his apostles' feet. The service also includes the "stripping of the altar," in which all items are removed from the altar in preparation for the observance of Good Friday.

Minister

The word *minister,* which comes from the Latin term meaning "servant," is commonly used for any ordained person. However, the term can describe anyone who ministers to—or helps—others. In the Anglican Church, all Christians are called to be ministers in the name of Christ. The Book of Common Prayer includes lay persons as ministers of the church.

Ministry

The Episcopal Book of Common Prayer defines Christian ministry as taking part "in the life, worship, and governance of the church" (page 855).

Over the years, the word *ministry* has come to mean the work of someone who is ordained, such as a priest or deacon. However, through baptism, all Christians are called to the ministry of Jesus. In baptism we become servants of God, a voice for God's love and forgiveness in the world.

Miracle

A miracle is an extraordinary event beyond human understanding. It is an act or occurrence achieved by God's grace, which may override the laws of nature.

The word *miracle* was first used in the twelfth century, but miraculous events were identified long before that time. Jesus performed many miracles during his ministry, including healing the sick and bringing the dead back to life. His first miracle was performed at the wedding at Cana, where he turned water into wine at the request of his mother (John 2:1–10):

> On the third day there was a wedding in Cana of Galilee and the mother of Jesus was there. Jesus and his disciples had also been invited to the wedding. When the wine gave out, the mother of Jesus said to him, "They have no wine." And Jesus said to her, "Woman, what concern is that to you and me? My hour has not yet come." His mother said to the servants, "Do whatever he tells you." Now standing there were six stone water-jars for the Jewish rites of purification, each holding twenty or thirty gallons. Jesus said to them, "Fill the jars with water." And they filled them up to the brim. "Now draw some out, and take it to the chief steward." So they

took it. When the steward tasted the water that had become wine, and did not know where it came from (though the servants who had drawn the water knew), the steward called the bridegroom and said to him, "Everyone serves the good wine first, and then the inferior wine after the guests have become drunk. But you have kept the good wine until now."

Mission

A mission is a local Anglican congregation that cannot support a full-time priest and so is not yet an official parish. Missions often serve small communities and may have limited services. They depend on the support of the local bishop, who may provide a part-time priest, called a vicar in the United States. While a parish is financially independent, a mission depends directly on the diocese for its financial support.

Movable Feast

Any church festival that doesn't fall on a fixed calendar day is called a movable feast—its actual date moves from year to year. Easter is the best example of a movable feast because the dates of many other feasts, such as Pentecost or Trinity Sunday, depend on when Easter is celebrated.

Nave (also look under Church Plan)

The word *nave* comes from the Latin word for "ship." In traditional church buildings, the nave is the large central space that crosses between the narthex and chancel. In late medieval times, the nave was separated from the main altar by a "rood screen." These screens were removed during the Reformation to bring the laypeople and the clergy closer together.

New Testament

The New Testament includes the books of Christian scripture in the Bible. These books include the four gospels, the Acts of the Apostles, a number of epistles (or letters) written by St. Paul and other writers to the early Christian communities. The New Testament ends with the book of Revelation.

Nicene Creed

The Nicene Creed is a statement of what Christians believe. Part of the text of the creed was written at the Council of Nicea, called by the Emperor Constantine in 325 CE (in the town of Nicea) in what is now Turkey. The creed developed out of the earliest baptismal promises Christians made when they joined the Church. In the Anglican Church, the Nicene Creed is usually recited during the Eucharist.

Offertory

The Offertory is the part of the Eucharist in which the bread and wine are presented for consecration at the altar. The offerings of the people—usually, the money placed on the collection plate—are also brought forward at this time. The act of presenting these gifts by representatives of the congregation is called the Offertory procession.

Old Testament

The Old Testament is the first part of the Holy Bible, written before the birth of Christ. It is also known as the Hebrew Scriptures. Revered by both Christians and Jews, it contains the Scriptures that detail the history of the Jewish people. These writings offer a pattern for holy living and chronicle the deepening relationship between God and his people. Christians believe that the Old Testament foretells the coming of Jesus Christ, the messiah promised by God. There are thirty-nine books in the Old Testament.

Orders, Religious

There are more than thirty religious orders in the Episcopal Church in the United States of America, and many more in the worldwide Anglican Communion. An order is a community of people who agree to live together and keep common vows or promises. Each community has a unique ministry, which may include hospitality, education, medical care, or spiritual guidance. Many members of religious orders wear special clothing called a habit.

Ordination

Ordination, or Holy Orders, is the sacrament by which Christians become bishops, priests, or deacons. The bishop lays hands on the newly ordained people, who promise to be loyal to the Church and to the teachings of Christ. The ordination ceremony usually takes place within the celebration of the Eucharist. The new ministers are presented to the bishop by the laypeople, who promise to help them in their new ministry.

Palm Sunday

Also known as the Passion Sunday, this day marks the beginning of Holy Week. It falls on the Sunday before Easter. In many churches, actual palm leaves are blessed and then distributed to the congregation in memory of Christ's triumphal entrance into Jerusalem, where he was cheered by crowds who would in a few days demand his execution. The Church procession on this day reenacts this event. In many parishes, the palm leaves are saved, then burned at a later time. The ashes from these leaves are sometimes placed on the foreheads of parishioners on Ash Wednesday.

Parable

Parables are short stories that describe a principal or important idea. Jesus often used parables in his teaching and many appear in the Bible. For example, in Luke's gospel Jesus is trying to explain to Simon Peter about debts (of sin), the mercy of God, and gratitude for forgiveness. He tells him a story (Luke 7:40–43):

> "A certain creditor had two debtors; one owed five hundred denarii, and the other fifty. When they

could not pay, he cancelled the debts for both of them. Now which of them will love him more?"

Simon answered, "I suppose the one for whom he cancelled the greater debt."

And Jesus said to him, "You have answered rightly."

Parish

A parish is a local congregation of Anglicans who worship together, help one another, participate in the sacraments, and encourage one another in the Christian life. A parish is usually made up of people who live within certain geographic boundaries, support a church building, and are served by a priest. In the United States, the priest in charge of the parish is known as the rector. In Canada, he or she is often known as the incumbent. The word *parish* comes from a Greek word meaning "neighbor."

A group of parishes within a certain geographic region make up a diocese.

Paschal Candle

This is a special large candle lit from a new fire at the beginning of the Easter Vigil. It is white and represents Christ's gift of light to the world. Along with a cross, the first and last letters of the Greek alphabet, the alpha and omega, are often inscribed upon the candle. This signifies that God is the eternal circle of life. The paschal candle burns throughout the Easter season, and is often lit during baptisms and funerals as well. In many parishes, the newly baptized child or adult is given a candle lit from the paschal candle.

Paschal Candle

Passover

This is the principal Jewish feast, which recalls the exodus of the Jewish people from Egypt where they were slaves. Jews throughout the world mark this event every year with a special meal called a seder. Jesus' last supper with his apostles, the night before his crucifixion, was the seder meal from which our Eucharist service evolved.

Pastor

The word *pastor* comes from a Latin word meaning "shepherd." This title is sometimes given to Anglican priests and clergy of other denominations because they are entrusted with following Jesus' command to Peter: *"Feed my lambs, feed my sheep."*

As pastors, clergy help people who are sick, in poverty, or grieving for those they have lost. They also look for ways to help those who have left the Church to return to its communion.

Paten

The paten is the round plate used to hold the bread of the Eucharist during the blessing and distribution of the communion.

Peace (exchange of)

The Christian tradition of exchanging the peace dates from the early years of the Church. In some early churches, in fact, people were required to exchange the peace before taking communion with members. Today this ritual greeting takes place

P   Pentecost

Sign of Peace

before the Eucharist, following the Liturgy of the Word. It usually involves a handshake or hug, and sometimes a kiss, and the words: *The peace of the Lord,* or *Peace be with you.*

Pentecost

The feast of Pentecost, fifty days after Easter, marks the end of the Easter season in the Church. On this day Christians remember the coming of the Holy Spirit to the apostles as they gathered in an upper room of a house in Jerusalem after Christ's ascension. Although they had been afraid to leave the house before this event, the Holy Spirit filled them with the courage to preach the gospel and to spread Jesus' "good news" throughout the world.

Baptisms are often performed during Pentecost. Because the newly baptized often wore white clothes, the day came to be called White Sunday, or Whitsun, in England and many other countries of the Anglican Communion. The word *Pentecost* comes from the Greek name for the Jewish Festival of Weeks.

Prayer

Prayer is our conversation with God. It can be formal or informal, spoken or sung, loud or silent. Prayer can be individual or communal. In the Anglican Church, ritual (liturgy) prayers were compiled in the Book of Common Prayer by Archbishop Thomas Cranmer in 1549. This book, revised many times over the years, is still the Church's official prayer book, although each member of the Anglican Communion creates its own particular set of prayers.

There are many different kinds of formal prayer. The Anglican Prayer Book, for example, contains a wide variety of prayers, including those for the morning (matins), the evening (vespers), and noontime. Christians also pray in their own words, offering thanks or praise, or asking forgiveness or help for themselves or others.

Presiding Bishop

The presiding bishop is the bishop elected to serve as head of the Episcopal Church in the U.S.A. The presiding bishop officiates at the ordination of bishops within the Church and presides over the House of Bishops when they meet every three years at the General Convention. The person holding this position is elected by the House of Bishops with agreement from the House of Deputies. This presiding bishop holds office for nine years and represents the Episcopal Church within the Anglican Communion.

The presiding bishop is also a symbol of the unity of the Episcopal dioceses in America, and represents the Episcopal Church within the Anglican Communion.

Primate

The primate is the bishop elected to serve as head of the Anglican Church of Canada. The primate presides over the House of Bishops (a gathering of all the Anglican bishops in Canada) when they meet several times a year. The primate also presides over the General Synod, which meets every three years. The person holding this position is elected by the General Synod, and serves until he or she retires. The primate represents the Anglican Church of Canada within the Anglican Communion and is a symbol of the Church's unity within Canada.

Priest

Priests are one of the three ordained orders of ministry in the church—bishops, priests, and deacons. They are ministers who serve the members of individual parishes in many different ways. They lead the celebration of the Eucharist, baptize people, preach sermons, and teach.

A priest in training goes through several steps. Those who feel called to the priesthood usually meet with representatives of the parish or diocese for initial approval. Then, they are asked to begin further education. Usually, this means three years of formal study at a theological college or seminary. All priests in training study the Bible, learn about the liturgy, and practice caring for the needs of the people. Often candidates receive pastoral training in parishes or other settings. During this period, candidates keep in close touch with their sponsoring bishop and diocese. When training is completed, candidates are ordained and begin to serve in a parish.

Procession

Procession

Processions are formal walks, usually within the church, by priests, deacons, servers, acolytes, and others. Sometimes church members participate, too. Processions typically take place at the beginning of the Sunday Eucharist, as the priest, acolytes, choir, and other ministers walk down the aisle to the altar. On Palm Sunday, Pentecost, and other major feast days, there may be special processions.

At the Eucharist service, bread and wine, along with the gifts of the people, are brought forward to the altar in the Offertory procession.

Province

In the Anglican Communion, a province is a group of dioceses within a geographic region. In the United States, for example, dioceses are grouped into nine provinces. In the Anglican Church of Canada, there are four provinces under the direction of an archbishop. Each province is under the direction of a bishop who acts as president of the province.

Psalms

Psalms are poems originally written in Hebrew. They appear in the Bible in a special book of the Old Testament.

Psalms are used in many different church services, especially the daily offices, which include all 150 psalms in a seven-week cycle of prayers. The psalms express every human emotion, from joy to grief, from anger to envy to gratitude, and place them all before a loving God. Psalms are prayed during every celebration of the Eucharist. They may be found in the Bible and in a special section of the Book of Common Prayer called the Psalter.

One of the most famous and beloved psalms is number 23, which begins: *The Lord is my shepherd; I shall not want.*

Pulpit

Pulpit comes from a Latin word meaning "platform." Similar to a lectern, it is a high stand, usually made of wood, from which a sermon is delivered. The gospel and the lessons may also be read from the pulpit. In many Anglican churches, the pulpit is adorned in front with a fabric hanging, or "pulpit fall," in the color of the liturgical season.

Purificator

The purificator, from the Latin words meaning "to make clean," is the small white linen cloth that the priest uses to wipe the rim of the chalice during the Eucharist service.

Reconciliation

Reconciliation is the forgiveness of sins. Christ forgave sins—often in the context of healing someone of physical illness. In the gospel of John (20:21–23), Jesus imparts this power to his apostles as he bestows the gifts of the Holy Spirit: . . . *As the father has sent me, so I send you. . . . Receive the Holy Spirit. If you forgive the sins of any, they are forgiven them; if you retain the sins of any, they are retained.*

The apostles in turn gave this power to those who followed them. In the Anglican Church, a priest offers absolution (pardon) to those who are sorry for their sins and seek forgiveness. Someone seeking forgiveness is called a penitent. In this way, Christians who become separated from God and from the church through sin can be forgiven and return to the church community. Anglicans recognize the Reconciliation of a Penitent as one of the sacramental rites of the church.

Rector (also look under Priest)

The word *rector* comes from the Latin word meaning "to lead" or "to rule." The rector is the leader of the parish and is accountable to the bishop.

Rectory

The rectory is the house where the rector lives. In many other Christian denominations, the clergy's residence is known as a manse or parsonage.

Reformation

The Reformation was a religious movement that took place in Europe during the sixteenth century. Those who took part in it wanted to reform—or change—some of the teachings and practices of the Roman Catholic Church. The Anglican Church grew out of the Reformation movement in England.

Requiem

A requiem is a formal Eucharist service for someone who has died. The word *requiem* has been used for such masses since the Middle Ages. It is part of the Latin phrase *requiem eternam,* meaning "eternal rest." In the Anglican Church, masses for the dead use the same liturgy as the one used at Easter. Vestments and church colors are white, focusing not so much on the grief of separation, but on the joy of eternal life.

Requiems also refer to church music composed for requiem masses. Many great pieces of classical music have been composed in this form, including Mozart's famous, unfinished *Requiem.*

Reverend

The title *reverend* is used for a member of the clergy such as a priest or deacon. For example, the official title of a priest might be the Reverend Dr. John Smith. In letters or in conversation, though, he should be called "Dr. Smith" or "Father Smith," according to his preference.

"The Right Reverend" is the formal title for a bishop in the Anglican Church. The term "Very Reverend" is used for the dean of a cathedral or seminary. "Most Reverend" is a term used for an archbishop, including the Archbishop of Canterbury, the Presiding Bishop of the United States, and the Primate of Canada.

Rite I and Rite II

The Episcopal Book of Common Prayer presents Anglican worship services in two formats, Rite I and Rite II. Rite I retains the older language of the 1928 version of the prayer book. Rite II contains the more contemporary language of the 1979 version.

Rubrics

Rubrics are directions in the Prayer Book for the way a particular worship service should be conducted. *Rubric* comes from the Latin word for red; these instructions are often printed in red to stand out in the text.

Sacrament

The word *sacrament* comes from a Latin word meaning "to consecrate" or "to make holy." For Anglicans, sacraments are "outward and visible signs of inward and spiritual grace, given by Christ as sure and certain means by which we receive that grace" (Book of Common Prayer, page 857). Through the sacraments, Christ has given the Church ways to bless important passages in human life.

In the Anglican Church there are two primary sacraments: baptism and Holy Eucharist. In baptism, the sign is water, and in the Eucharist, it is bread and wine. There are five other sacramental rites: ordination, confirmation, reconciliation, marriage, and anointing.

Seminary

The word *seminary* comes from the Latin word for "seed." A seminary is a school where people are trained and educated to become priests. In the Anglican Church, priests are usually required to be graduates of a seminary or theological college, where they receive a master's degree in divinity.

Septuagint (look under Apocrypha)

Sequence Hymn

On some important feast days, such as Easter and Pentecost, a special hymn is sung or recited. It is called a sequence because it follows immediately after the Epistle reading. The name comes from the Latin word meaning "to follow."

Sign of the Cross

The sign of the cross is a physical reminder of Christian identity. The sign of the cross can be used in a number of different ways. It can be signed upon oneself—touching the forehead, the heart, then the left and right shoulder. The sign is also used during baptism, confirmation, or an anointing, when the priest, with his thumb, traces a cross on the forehead of the recipient. The sign of the cross is also used by the priest in giving blessings and in forgiving sins. At the end of the celebration of the Eucharist, the priest uses an outward sign of the cross to bless the congregation.

Sign of Cross

Stations of the Cross

This is a devotional practice that commemorates fourteen events, or "stations," leading up to Jesus' crucifixion and resurrection. Some Anglican churches contain pictures or other artwork depicting these stations along the side walls of the nave.

The stations of the cross are often followed during Lent, either individually or communally, especially on Good Friday.

Stole (also look under **Vestments**)

A stole is a long band of fabric, usually matching the liturgical color of the day or season, worn by a bishop, priest, or deacon during the celebration of the Eucharist. The stole is worn in a specific way by different types of clergy. A priest wears it with the ends hanging straight down; a deacon wears it diagonally across the chest, as a symbol of obedience to Christ.

Surplice (also look under **Vestments**)

The surplice, usually white, is a full, knee-length vestment worn over the cassock. Worn by both clergy and lay eucharistic ministers, the surplice came into use during medieval times.

Stole and Surplice

Tabernacle

The tabernacle is a small, sometimes highly decorated container where the consecrated communion bread is stored when it is not being used. The consecrated bread and wine is called the reserved sacrament because it has been reserved or put away to use at another time. The word comes from the name of a tent sanctuary used by the Israelites during the Exodus—the flight from Egypt.

Tabernacle

Tenebrae

The tenebrae, which comes from the Latin word meaning "darkness," is a special evening service held during Holy Week, usually on Wednesday. During this service, fifteen candles are lit and then, one by one, each candle is extinguished until only one burning candle remains. As that candle is hidden, the church is plunged into darkness. At the same time a loud noise is made symbolizing the earthquake at the time of Jesus' death on the cross as recorded by Matthew (27:50–54). Then the last candle is brought back in, so that worshipers can leave the church by its light.

> Then Jesus cried again with a loud voice and breathed his last. At that moment the curtain of the temple was torn in two from top to bottom. The earth shook, and the rocks were split. . . . Now when the centurion and those with him who were keeping watch over Jesus saw the earthquake and what took

place, they were terrified and said, "Truly this man was God's son."

Thirty-nine Articles (look under **Articles of Religion**)

Thurible (also look under **Incense**)

Also called an incense boat or a censer, this is a device for burning incense. It consists of a lidded metal container suspended by a chain. The lid of the container has holes for the incense smoke to escape. The chain is used to swing the container back and forth while the incense burns.

Three-Legged Stool

Anglicans use the image of a three-legged stool to describe their approach to the Christian life. The legs are Scripture (the Bible), tradition (the writings of the bishops and other Church leaders through the centuries), and reason.

Tithe

Tithe is an Old English word for the fraction one-tenth. To tithe is to give ten percent of one's income, or wealth, to the church. The principle of tithing comes from the Old Testament. In Genesis, Jacob (Isaac's son) promises God a tithe, or a tenth of all he receives. Among the Israelites, faith required a Jew to give an offering of a tenth of all animals and fruits of the land. Anglicans are asked to assist in the work of the church, but no specific amount of money is demanded. The general support of the church, through time and talents as well as through money, is known as "stewardship."

Transept (also look under **Church Plan**)

In traditional churches, which are cross-shaped, the transept is the part of the church forming the horizontal bar, usually running north to south. The aisle in front of the first pew, which separates the nave from the chancel, is also called the transept.

Triduum

Triduum is Latin for "three days of prayer." In the Anglican Church, it usually refers to the three days before Easter: Maundy Thursday, Good Friday, and the Easter Vigil.

Unction

This term comes from the Latin word meaning "to anoint." A priest may anoint a sick person with holy oil in order to bring the healing or the comfort of Christ.

Verger

Verger comes from a French word meaning "rod." In the Anglican Church, the verger carries a ceremonial staff or rod during important processions. The verger is also responsible for the care of the inside of the church building.

Vespers

Vespers, which comes from a Latin word that means "evening," was traditionally the first hour of prayer in monasteries. Now it refers to part or all of evening prayer.

Vestments

Vestments are the clothing worn by both the clergy and lay leaders during worship. Many of the vestments worn during services are adaptations of ancient Roman street clothing. The basic vestment is a long neck-to-ankle covering called a cassock. Priests and deacons wear a black cassock; bishops, as well as archdeacons, wear purple. Cassocks are sometimes worn alone, but more often are covered with the surplice, a full knee-length white vestment with wide sleeves. (The cotta is similar to a surplice, but shorter. It is often worn by choir members and acolytes.)

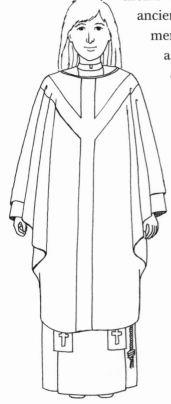

Vested Priest

Another common vestment is the alb, a full-length white or off-white tunic, usually gathered at the waist by a rope or cincture. The alb is worn at the altar by the person celebrating the Eucharist as well as by other ministers. The chasuble is an outer garment that priests and bishops wear over the alb when celebrating the Eucharist. The stole, another vestment, is a long, narrow band of fabric in a color representing the church season. Stoles are worn by priests, bishops, and deacons. Deacons also wear a full-length covering called a dalmatic.

Vestry

Vestry members along with the clergy are responsible for organizing and managing the church. In Canada, this group of people is often referred to as an advisory board, a parish council, or a vestry board.

The number of vestry, or board, members varies from parish to parish. Each member is nominated and then elected by the members of the church and serves for a given term. Often a specific member will have responsibility over a particular aspect of how the church operates. For instance, an accountant might oversee parish finances, while a carpenter might take charge of building maintenance and repair.

The vestry or board oversees the way church resources are used. When planning the budget, they look at church-sponsored activities including educational programs, such as lectures or films, or social programs, such as soup kitchens or homeless shelters. Together the vestry decides how to fund these activities in a way best suited to the community.

The word *vestry* has the same root as "vestments." It comes from the Latin "to clothe." The room where the priest put on vestments for the Eucharist used to be called the vestry; parishioners used to meet in this room to discuss church business.

Via Media

This is a Latin phrase that means "the middle way." It refers to the Anglican quest to find a middle ground between Roman Catholic focus on the teachings of the pope and bishops, and the Protestant reliance on Scripture. Instead, Anglicans seek a middle way by finding God through Scripture, reason, and tradition.

Vicar

In the United States, a vicar is a priest who leads a mission or a congregation that depends on the diocese for its resources. The vicar is appointed by the bishop and reports to him or her. In England, the vicar is the title of the priest in charge of a congregation.

Vows

Vows are solemn agreements or promises made in the presence of witnesses. The first vows for an Anglican take place at baptism when the infant's parents and godparents promise (in the child's name) to keep the Christian faith. Later, during confirmation, the child, now a teenager, repeats these vows for him- or herself. Adults may take further vows; for example, they may take marriage vows; those becoming priests and deacons take ordination vows. Members of Anglican religious orders take vows committing themselves to serve Christ and his Church as brothers or sisters.

Warden

A warden is an official of a parish and takes a leadership role in the parish council or vestry. Some wardens are chosen by the parish priest; they are called senior wardens in the United States and rector's wardens in Canada. Some wardens are elected by the lay people of the parish and are sometimes known as people's wardens. Wardens always hold positions of leadership in a parish, though their duties vary from diocese to diocese.

Whitsunday (look under Pentecost)

World Council of Churches (also look under Ecumenism)

This group of churches, of which the Anglican Church is a part, was founded in Amsterdam, the Netherlands, in 1948. Its purpose was to work toward unity among Christian churches, including the possibility of shared sacraments. The W.C.C. now includes over 400 churches in 120 countries on every continent, representing some 400 million Christians.